Black Sabbath
Anthology

Amsco Publications
New York/London/Sydney

Front cover photo by James Shive/Retna Ltd.
Arrangements and solo transcriptions by Mark Phillips
Edited by Peter Pickow

This book Copyright © 1986 by Amsco Publications
A Division of Music Sales Corporation, New York, NY.

Order No. AM 62019
US International Standard Book Number: 0.8256.1084.2
UK International Standard Book Number: 0.7119.0846.X

Exclusive Distributors:
Music Sales Corporation
257 Park Avenue South, New York, NY 10010 USA
Music Sales Limited
8/9 Frith Street, London W1V 5TZ England
Music Sales Pty. Limited
120 Rothschild Street, Rosebery, Sydney, NSW 2018, Australia

Printed in the United States of America by
Vicks Lithograph and Printing Corporation

NOVEMBER 2014

Legend of Musical Symbols 4

A Hard Road 12

A National Acrobat 7

Black Sabbath 17

Children of the Grave 20

Children of the Sea 25

Country Girl 30

Dirty Women 37

Fairies Wear Boots/Jack The Stripper 45

Heaven and Hell 50

Iron Man 56

Junior's Eyes 62

Looking for Today 69

N.I.B. 74

Neon Knights 78

Never Say Die 84

Paranoid 89

Planet Caravan 92

Sabbath, Bloody Sabbath 96

Sleeping Village/A Bit of Finger 100

Snowblind 104

Supernaut 108

Sweet Leaf 34

Tomorrow's Dream 42

Under the Sun/Every Day Comes and Goes 112

Voodoo 66

War Pigs 116

The Wizard 124

LEGEND OF MUSICAL SYMBOLS

T
A
B
The six lines of the tablature staff represent the six strings of the guitar, with the top line representing the high E. The numbers designate the frets to be played. A zero represents an open string.

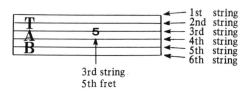

H **Hammer-on:** Play the first note normally, then strike the second (higher) note with a finger of the left hand.

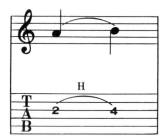

P **Pull-off:** Play the first note normally, then pull off the left-hand finger from the string to sound the second (lower) note, which should already be in position.

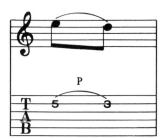

B **Bend: Type 1/Fast Bend:** Finger the lower note indicated, then quickly bend the string until you achieve the sound of the higher note.

Bend: Type 2/Slow Bend: This is executed in the same manner as the **Fast Bend**, but the string is bent in the rhythm indicated.

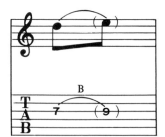

R   **Reverse Bend: Type 1/Fast Reverse Bend:** Finger the lower note indicated, but before striking the string bend it so that the higher note will sound. After striking the string, quickly release the bend and the lower note will sound.

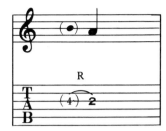

Reverse Bend: Type 2/Slow Reverse Bend: This is executed in the same manner as the **Fast Reverse Bend**, but the bend is released in the rhythm.

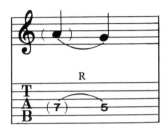

UB   **Unison Bend:** A unison on adjacent strings is produced by fingering the note indicated on the lower string and then quickly bending that string to the pitch of the unbent note played on the higher string.

S   **Slide: Type 1/From a definite pitch to another definite pitch:** Play the first note normally, then slide the left-hand finger to the second note.

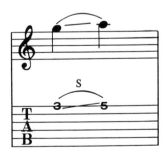

Slide: Type 2/From an indefinite pitch to a definite pitch: If the slanted line ascends, slide up to the note indicated from a few frets below. If the slanted line descends, slide down to the note from a few frets above.

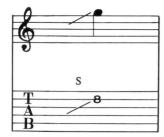 

Slide: Type 3/From an indefinite pitch to an indefinite pitch: If the slanted line ascends, slide up from the note indicated, but lift your finger after moving up a few frets. If the slanted line descends, slide down from the note, but lift your finger after moving down a few frets.

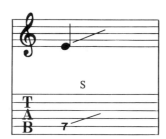 

Vibrato: Quickly move the string back and forth with a finger of the hand.

Downstroke

Upstroke

Accent: An accent above or below a note tells you to play the note louder.

Staccato: A dot above or below a note tells you to play the note short.

A NATIONAL ACROBAT

Words and Music by Frank Iommi, William Ward, Terence Butler, and John Osbourne

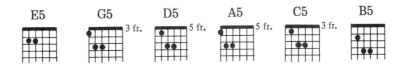

I am the world that hides the u-ni-ver-sal se-cret of all time.
When lit-tle worlds col-lide, I'm trapped in-side my em-bry-on-ic cell,

De-struc-tion of the emp-ty spac-es is my one and on-ly crime.
And flash-ing mem-o-ries are cast in-to the nev-er-end-ing well.

I've lived a thou-sand times. I found out what it means to be be-lieved.
The name that scorns the face, the child that nev-er sees the cause of man,

The thoughts and im-ag-es, the un-born child that nev-er was con-ceived.
The death-ly dark-ness that be-

lies the fate of those who nev-er

*To play along with the recording, tune all the strings down one whole step.
**E5 = E(omit 3rd).

1. ran.
2. (vocal tacet)

You've got - ta be - lieve_ me.
I want you to lis - ten.

Figure 2 (2 bars)

Continue Fig. 2 for 10 bars

I'm talk - ing to you._
I'm try'n' - a get through._
Well, I know it's hard for you to know the
Love has giv - en life to you and now it's

rea - son why._
your con - cern._
And I know you'll un - der - stand more when it's time to die._
Un - seen eyes of in - ner life will make your soul re - turn._

Don't be - lieve the life you have will be the on - ly one._
Still I look, but not to touch. The seeds of life are sown._

You have to let your bod - y sleep to let your soul live on._
The cur - tain of the fu - ture falls; the se - cret stays un - known._

Solo
N.C.

Backing Guitar plays Fig. 2 throughout Solo

Just re-mem-ber love is life,__ and hate is
Look-ing back, I've lived and learned,__but now I'm

liv - ing death.
won-der-ing.

Treat your life, for what it's worth__ and live for
Here I wait, and on - ly guess__ what this next

1.

ev - 'ry breath.

2.

life will bring.

Ha ha!__

*Indicates note played by Bass Guitar only

Play 4 times

A HARD ROAD

Words and Music by Anthony Iommi, Terence Butler, John Osbourne, and William Ward

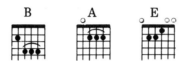

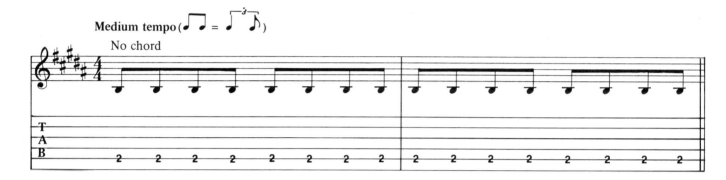

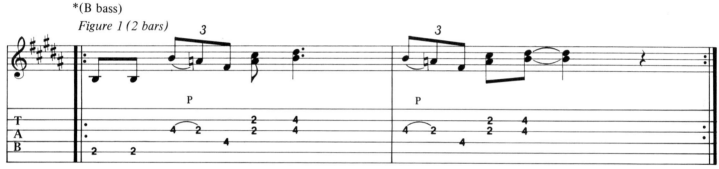

Play 3 times

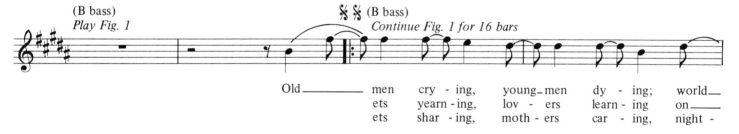

Old ____ men cry - ing, young men dy - ing; world ____
ets yearn - ing, lov - ers learn - ing on ____
ets shar - ing, moth - ers car - ing, night -

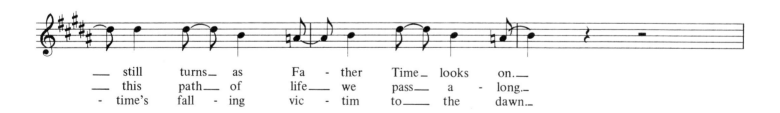

____ still turns____ as Fa - ther Time____ looks on.____
____ this path____ of life____ we pass____ a - long.____
- time's fall - ing vic - tim to____ the dawn.____

On ____ and on.____   Chil -
Is ____ it wrong.____   Wid -
Shad - ows mourn.____   Days

* Indicates note played by Bass Guitar only

dren play - ing, dream - ers pray - ing; laugh - ter turns_ to tears;_
ows weep - ing, ba - bies sleep - ing, life _ be - comes_ the sing -
_ are fall - ing, time_ is call - ing; to_ the earth an - oth -

_ love_ has gone. Has it gone?
er and_ the song._ Sing_ a - long._
er life_ is born._ Love_ lies drawn._

B   A
1. Oh,_____ it's a hard _____ road._
2.3. Oh,_____ it's a hard _____ road._

E   A   B   *To Coda II* A   1.   E   A
Oh,_____ it's a hard _____ road._
Car - ry your

(B bass)
Play Fig. 1 for 4 bars

Po

2.
A   E   A   (B bass)
own _____ load._____

T
A
B   2 2 2 2 2 2 2 2   2 2 2 2 2 2   4 4

14

Solo
(B bass)

Backing Guitar plays Fig. 1 for 8 bars

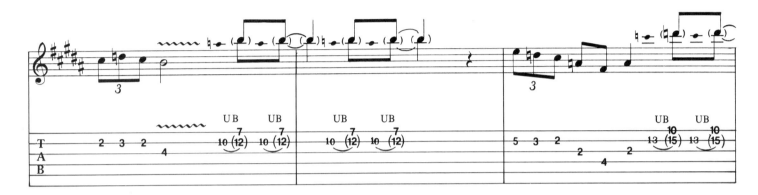

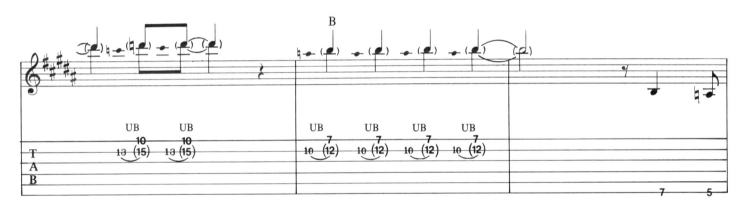

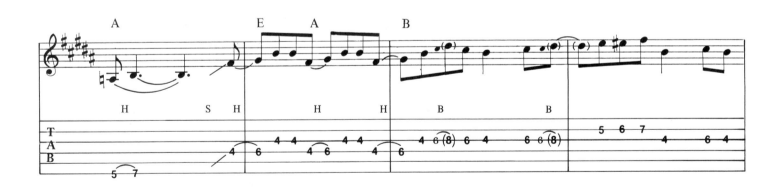

BLACK SABBATH

Words and Music by Frank Iommi, Terence Butler, William Ward, and John Osbourne

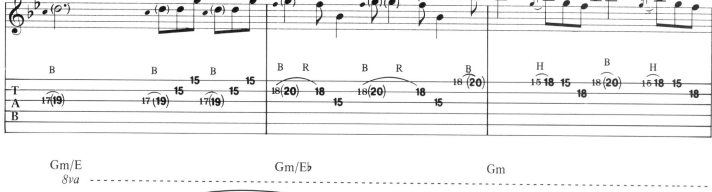

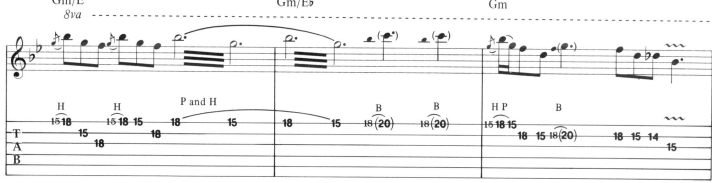

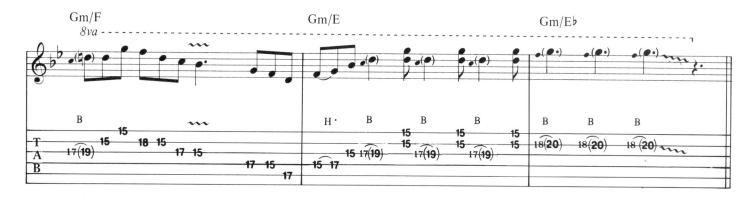

Play 3 times

*G5 = G (omit 3rd)

CHILDREN OF THE GRAVE

Words and Music by Frank Iommi, William Ward, John Osbourne, and Terence Butler

*To play along with recording, tune all strings down one whole step.

**C5 = C(omit 3rd)

22

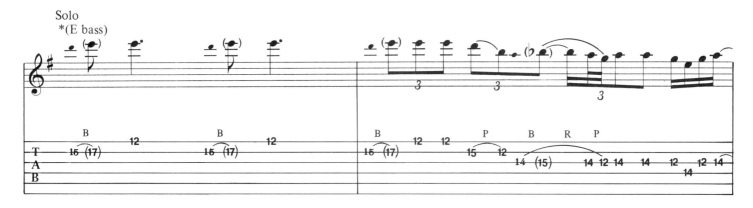

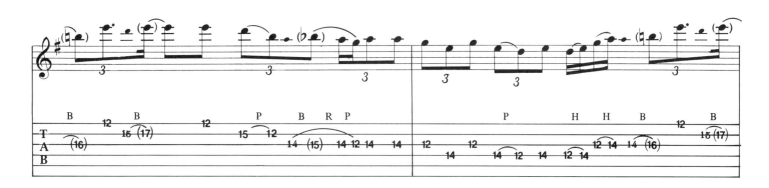

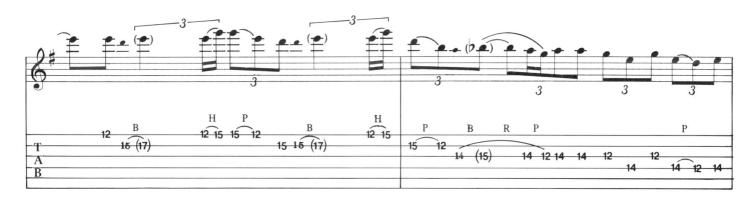

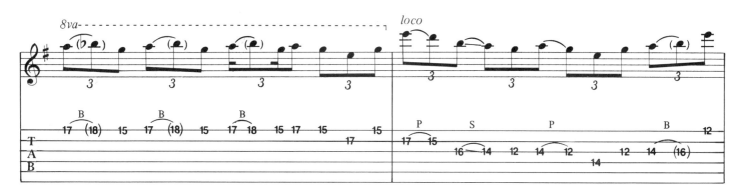

*Indicates note played by Bass Guitar only.

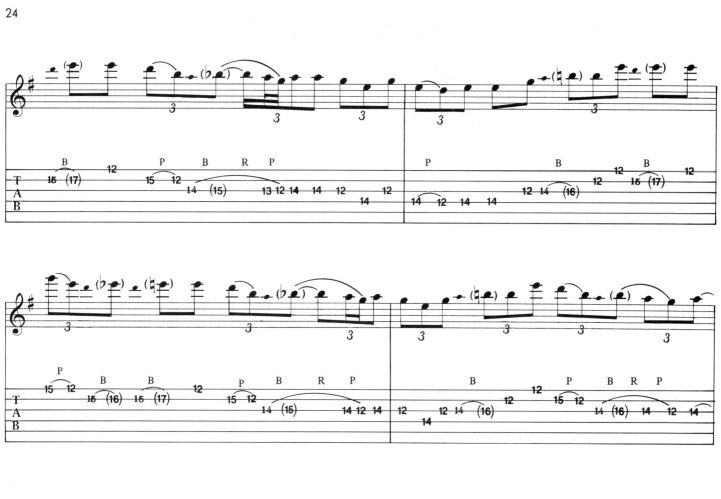

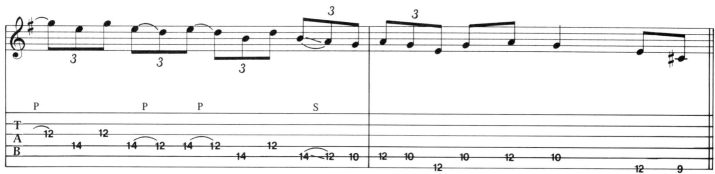

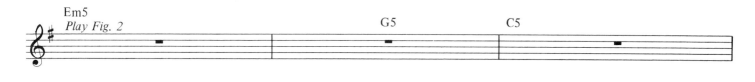

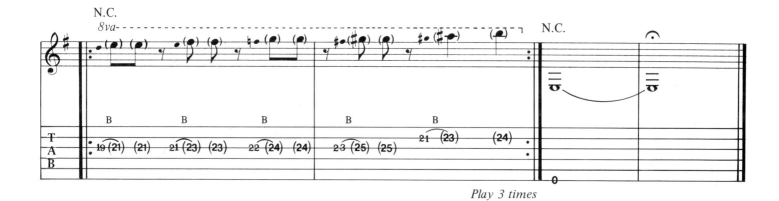

Play 3 times

CHILDREN OF THE SEA

**Words by Ronnie James Dio/Music by Ronnie James Dio, Terence Butler,
Anthony Iommi, and William Ward**

26

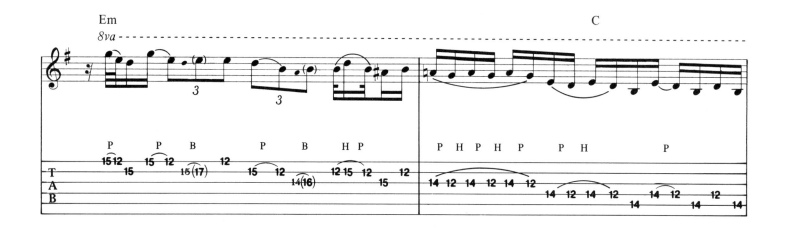

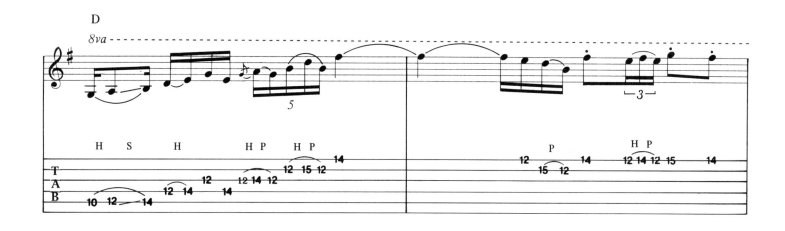

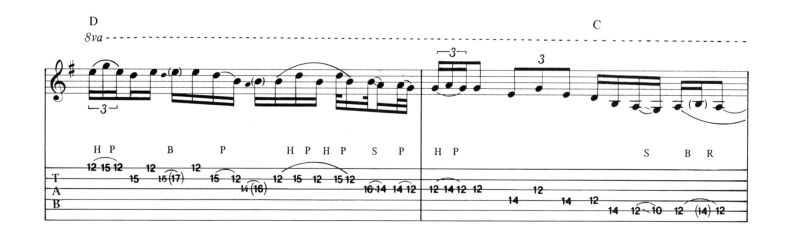

COUNTRY GIRL

Words by Ronnie James Dio/Music by Terry Butler, Ronnie James Dio, and Tony Iommi

We

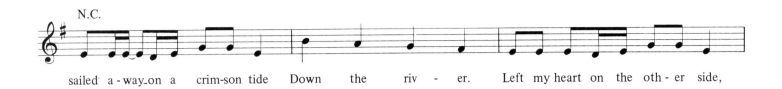

sailed a-way on a crim-son tide Down the riv - er. Left my heart on the oth - er side,

all to break it in - to bits. Her smile was a win - ter song, a Sab -bath end - ing.

Don't sleep or you'll find me gone, just an im - age in the

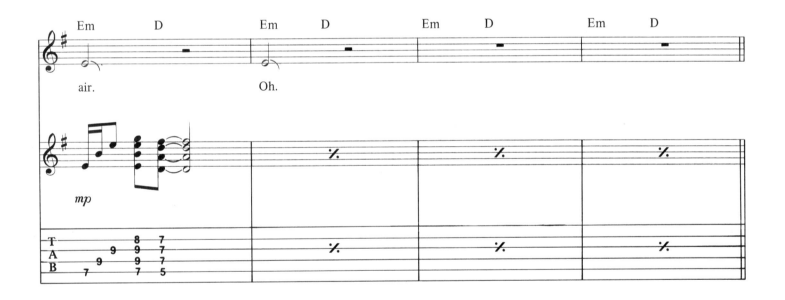

air. Oh.

In dreams I think of you.

Figure 3 (2 bars)

*D5=D (omit 3rd)

I don't know what to do with my - self.____

Time has left me down. She brings

bro - ken dreams,__ fall - ing stars,__ the end - less search__ for where you are,_____

So wrong, ____ so wrong,__ so wrong,____ so - wrong.__

Solo
N.C.
Backing Guitar plays Fig. 1

SWEET LEAF

Words and Music by Frank Iommi, William Ward, John Osbourne, and Terence Butler

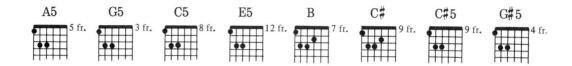

All right now.
I love you.
Come on now.

Won't you lis - ten?
Oh, you know it.
Try it out.____

When I____ first met you,   did - n't re - al - ize,____   I can't for -
My life____ was emp - ty,   for - ev - er on a down,____   Un - til you
Straight peo - ple don't know   what you're a - bout.____   They put you

get you   or your sur - prise.____   You in - tro - duced me   to my
took me,   showed me a - round.____   My life is free now;   my life is
down____   and shut you out.____   You gave to me____   a new to -

mind____   And left me watch - ing   you and your kind.____   Oh____ yeah.
clear.____   I love you, Sweet Leaf,   though you can't hear.____   Oh____ yeah.
day,____   And soon the world____   will love you, Sweet Leaf.   Oh____ yeah.

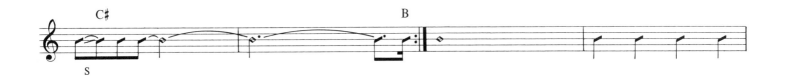

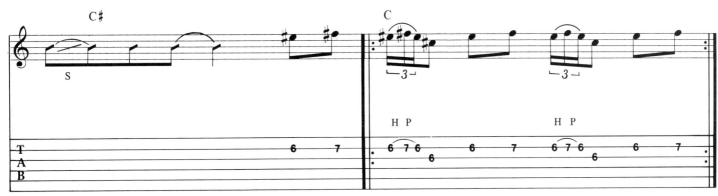

*A5 = A (omit 3rd)

Play 4 times

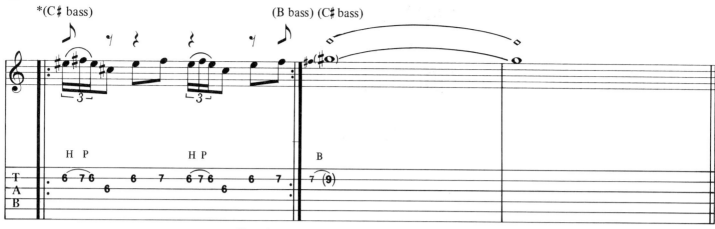

Play 4 times

*Indicates note played by Bass Guitar only

Repeat and fade

DIRTY WOMEN

Words and Music by Frank Iommi, Terence Butler, William Ward, and John Osbourne

38

* Indicates note played by Bass Guitar only
** Right channel overdub not notated

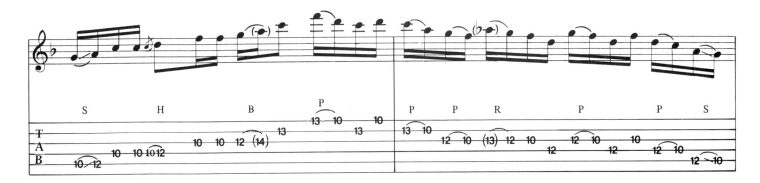

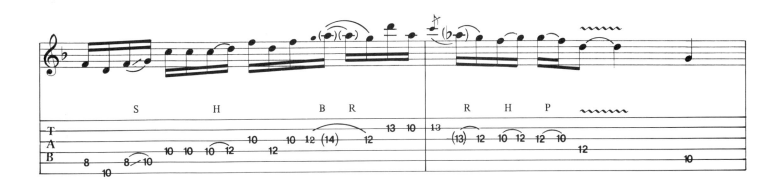

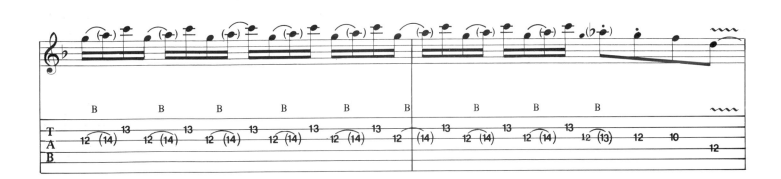

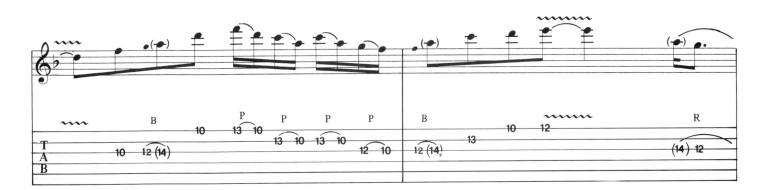

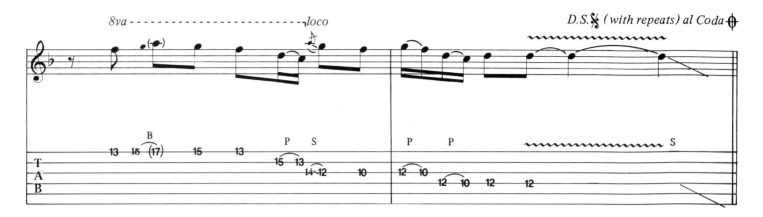

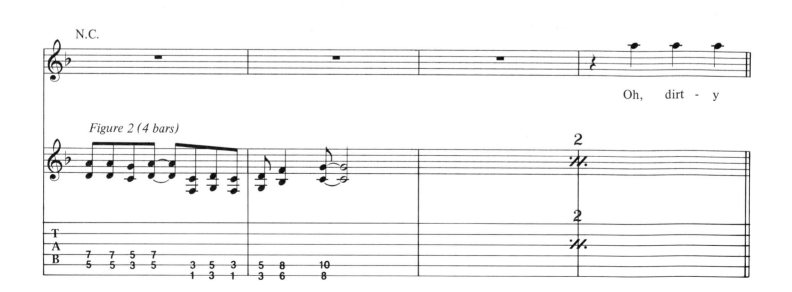

TOMORROW'S DREAM

Words and Music by Frank Iommi, Terence Butler, William Ward, and John Osbourne

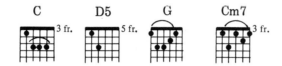

Medium rock beat

leav - ing to - mor - row at day - break; Catch the

fast - est train a - round nine. Yes, I'm leav - ing the sor - row and heart -

ache Be - fore it takes me a - way from my mind.

Solo

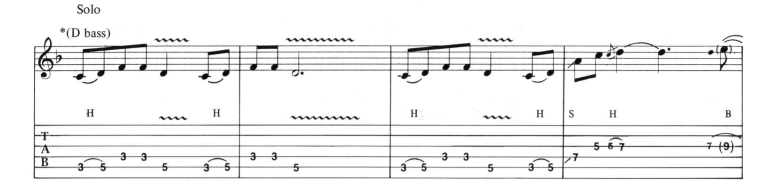

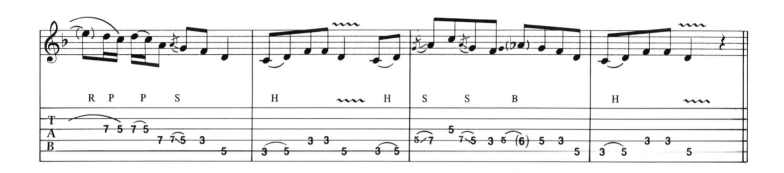

So re - al - ize I'm much bet - ter with - out___ you. You're not the

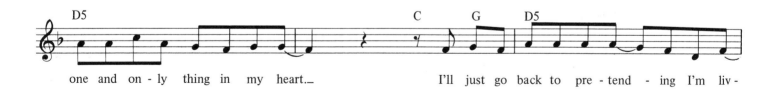

one and on - ly thing in my heart.___ I'll just go back to pre - tend - ing I'm liv -

ing, So this time I'm gon - na have to de - part.___

Play 3 times

* Indicates note played by Bass Guitar only

Medley:
FAIRIES WEAR BOOTS/JACK THE STRIPPER

Words and Music by Frank Iommi, John Osbourne, William Ward, and Terence Butler

46

Continue Fig. 1 for 16 bars
(on D.S. play Fig. 2 for 16 bars)

Fair-ies wear boots,— and you got-ta be-lieve— me.

Yeah, I saw— it, I saw— it. I tell— you no lies.—

Yeah, fair-ies wear boots,— and you got-ta be-lieve— me.

I saw it, I saw— it with my

To Coda

own two eyes.————— Whoa,— right— now.

Solo
*(G bass)

(G bass)

*Indicates note played by Bass Guitar only.

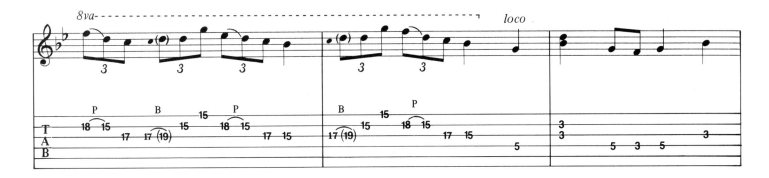

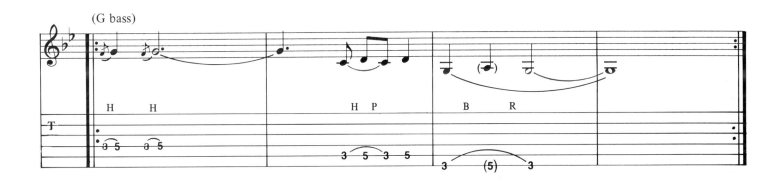

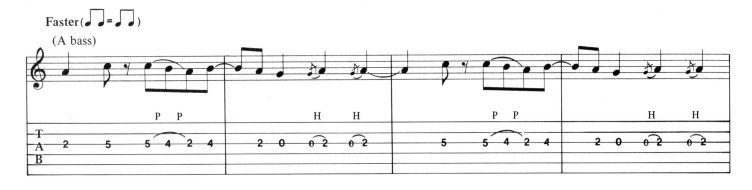

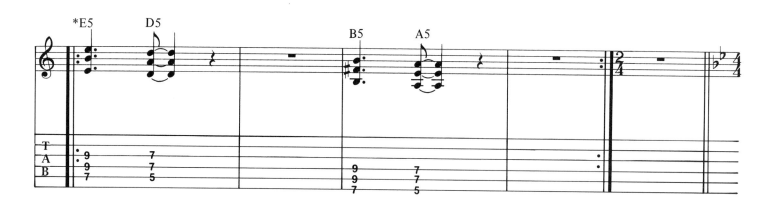

*E5 = E(omit 3rd)

Repeat and fade

HEAVEN AND HELL

**Words by Ronnie James Dio/Music by Ronnie James Dio, Terence Butler,
Anthony Iommi, and William Ward**

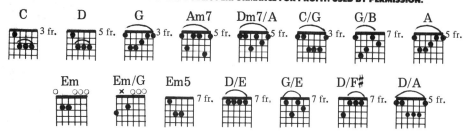

Moderately

N.C.

Figure 1 (8 bars)

Figure 2 (4 bars)
Bass part adapted for Guitar

Continue Fig. 2 for 8 bars

Sing me a song;___ you're a sing - er.
lov - er of life's___ not a sin - ner.
seems to be real,___ it's il - lu - sion. The

Do me a wrong;___ you're a bring - er of e - vil. The
end - ing is just___ a be - gin - ner. The
mo - ment of truth___ there's con - fu - sion in life.___

*Indicates note played by Bass Guitar only

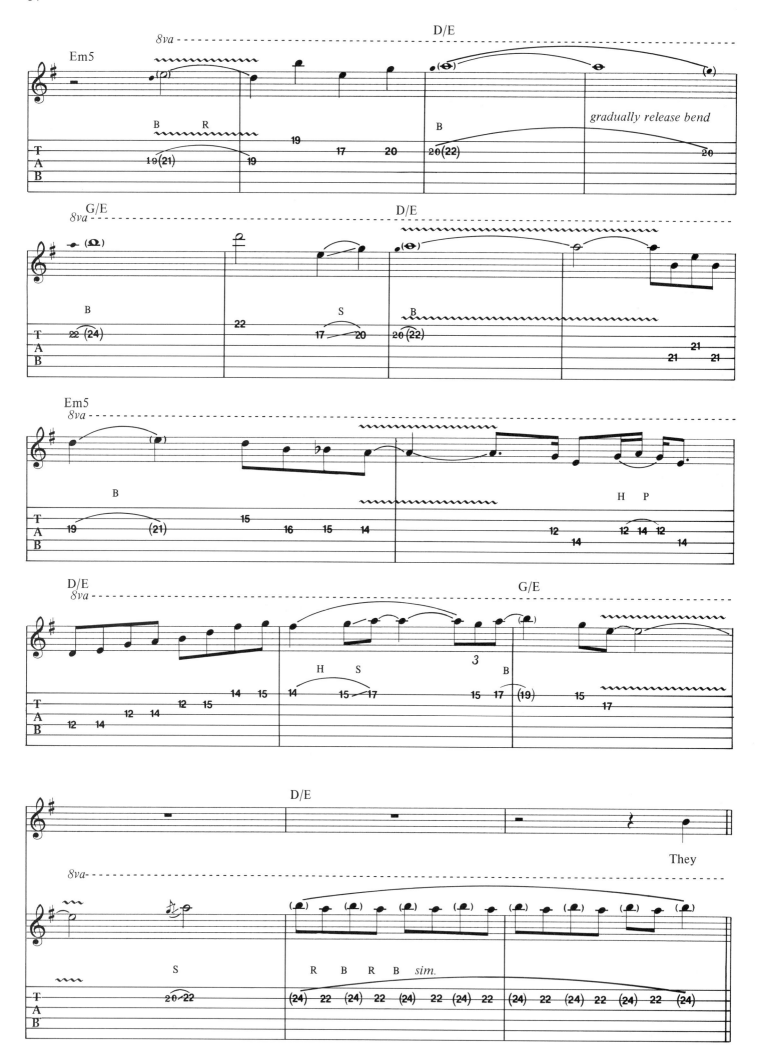

IRON MAN

Words and Music by Frank Iommi, John Osbourne, William Ward, and Terence Butler

world.
heads.

Plan - ning his ven - geance_ geance_
No - bod - y helps_ him._

that he will_ soon un -
Now he has_ his re -

fold.
venge.

* Indicates note played by Bass Guitar only

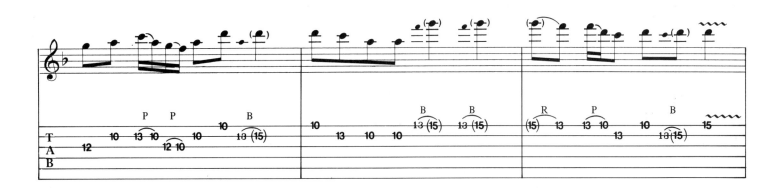

End of Solo

Tempo I

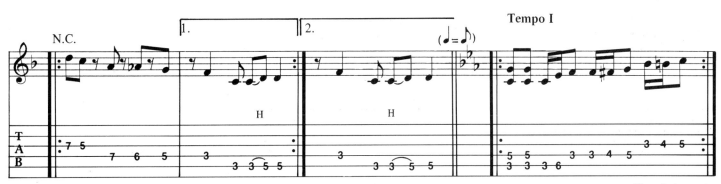

Play 4 times

Play Fig. 1 for 4 bars

Play Fig. 4 for 4 bars

Heav - y bolts of lead, fills_ his_ vic - tims full of dread.

Run - ning as fast as they can, I - ron_ Man_ lives a - gain.

1.2. 3.

Double time

(F bass)

(F bass)

(Eb bass) (D bass) (Db bass)

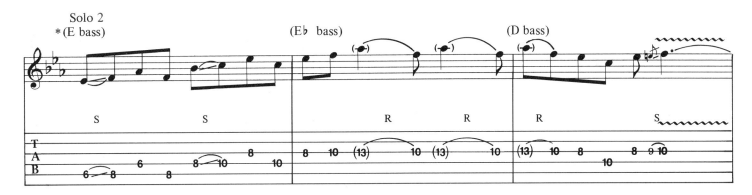

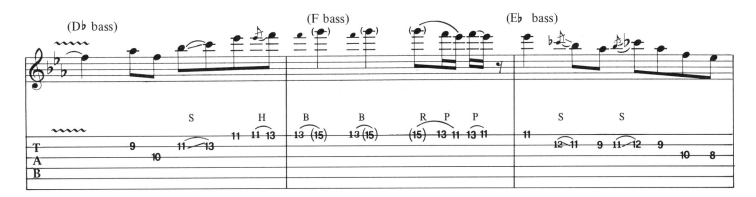

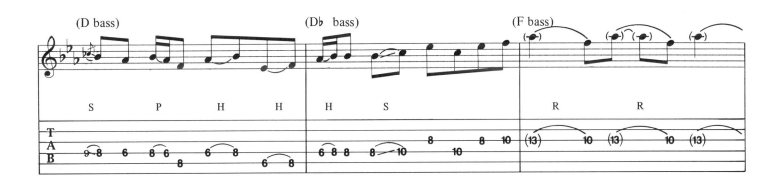

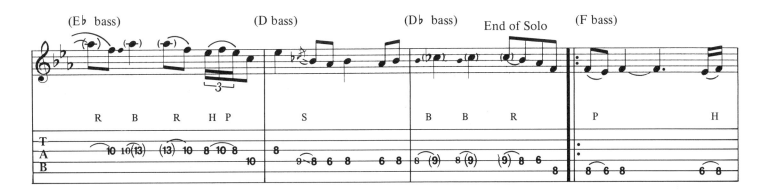

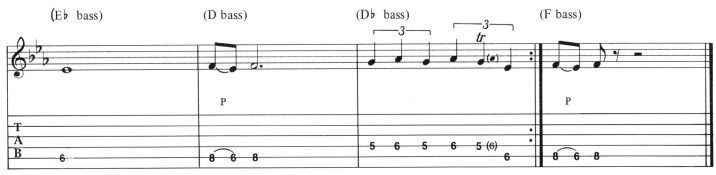

* Left channel overdub not notated

Play 3 times

JUNIOR'S EYES

Words and Music by Anthony Iommi, Terence Butler, John Osbourne, and William Ward

*Bass part adapted for guitar

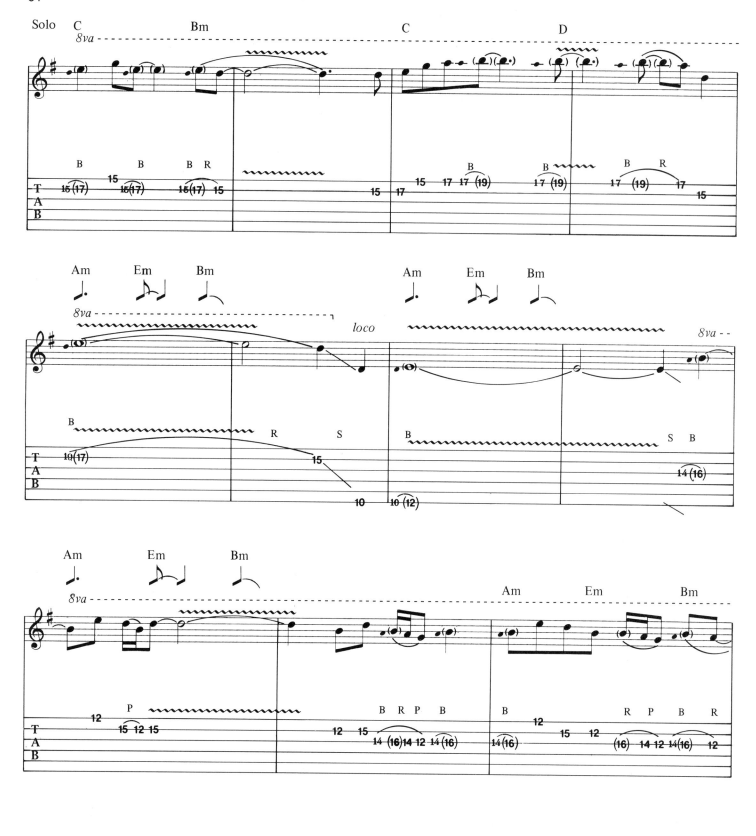

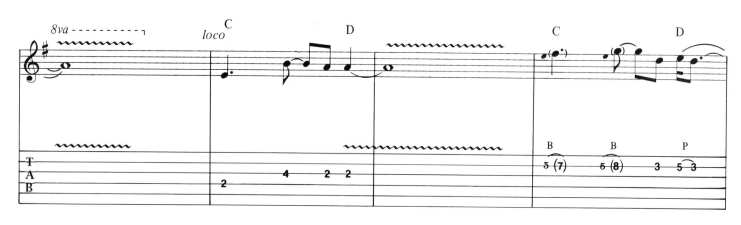

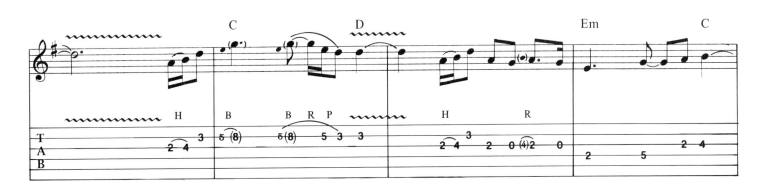

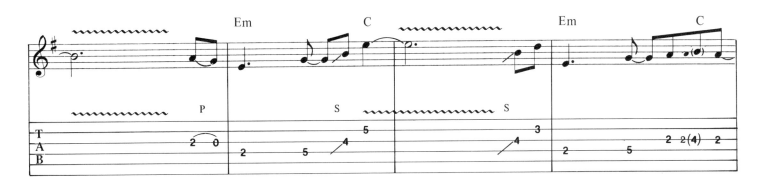

* E5 = E (omit 3rd)

VOODOO

Words by Ronnie James Dio/Music by Terry Butler, Ronnie James Dio, and Tony Iommi

Say you don't love__ me, you burn.__ You can re-fuse,__ but you lose,__

__ it's by me. Say you don't love__ me, you learn.__

Noth-ing you do__ will re-new__ 'cause I'm through.

Call me a li-ar, you knew.__ You were a fool,__ but that's cool,__ it's all right.
Fade in-to shad-ow, you burn.__ Your for-tune is free;__ I can see__ it's no good.

Call me the dev - il, it's true.__ Some can't ac - cept,__ but I crept__
Nev - er look back,_nev - er turn.__ It's a ques -tion of time__ till you're mine__

— in - side you. So if a stran - ger calls__ you,
— and you learn. So if a stran - ger sees__ you,

don't let him whis-per his name,_'cause it's voo - doo.__
don't look in his eyes__'cause he's voo - doo.__

Voo-doo.

Bring me your chil-dren, they'll burn.

Nev - er look back,_ nev - er turn.___

Cry me a riv - er, you

learn. Voo-doo.___

Repeat and fade

LOOKING FOR TODAY

Words and Music by Frank Iommi, William Ward, Terence Butler, and John Osbourne

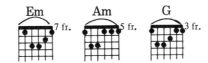

It's com-plete, but ob-so-lete. All to-mor-rows be-come yes-ter day.
Don't de-lay; you're in to-day, but to-mor-row is an-oth-er dream.
Glam-our trip so soon to slip. Eas-y come, but oh how quick it goes.

In de-mand, but sec-ond-hand, it's been heard
Sun-day's star is Mon-day's scar; out of date
Ten foot tall, but what a fall; hard to o-

be-fore you e-ven play. Up to date, but
be-fore you're e-ven seen. At the top, so
pen yet so eas-y to close. Front page news, but

came too late. Bet-ter get your-self an-oth-er name.
quick to flop, you're so new but rot-ting in de-cay.
so a-bused. You just want to hide your-self a-way.

* To play along with recording, tune all strings down one whole-step.

*D5 = D(omit third)

** This two-bar vocal pattern continues during Solo, but fades out after 14 bars.

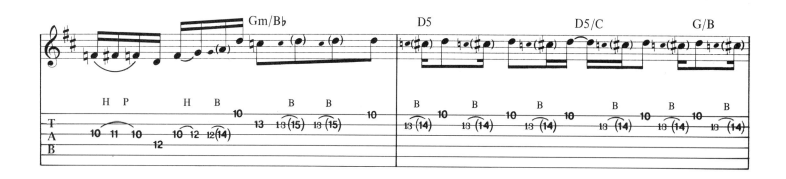

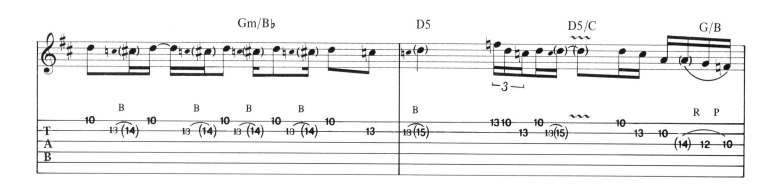

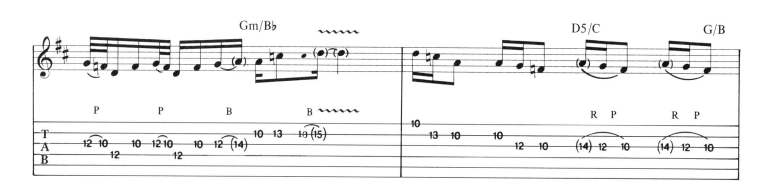

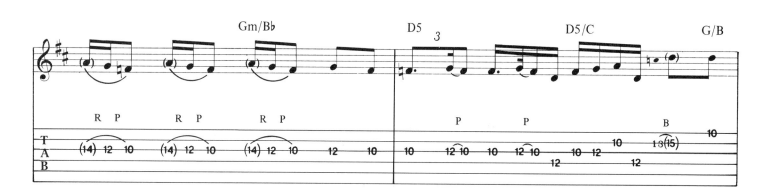

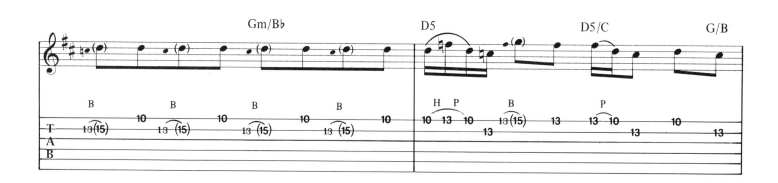

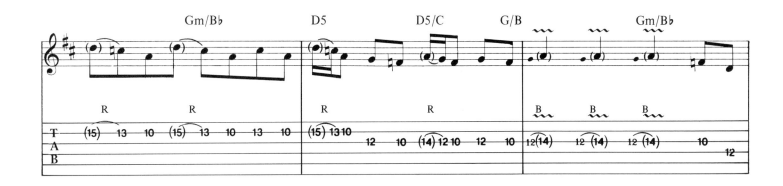

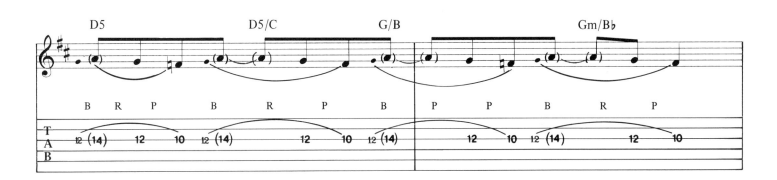

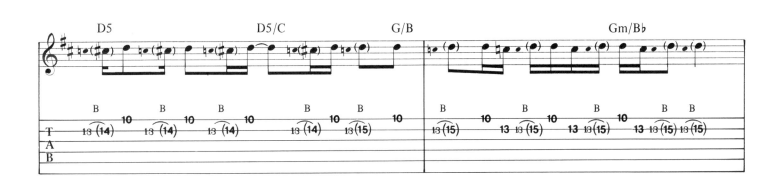

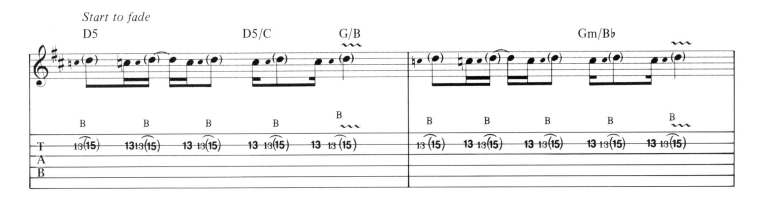

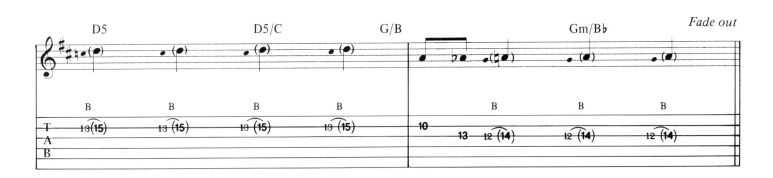

N.I.B.

Words and Music by Frank Iommi, Terence Butler, William Ward, and John Osbourne

*E5=E(omit 3rd)

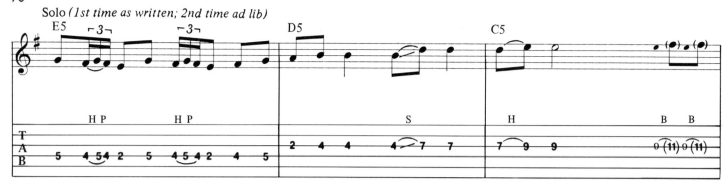

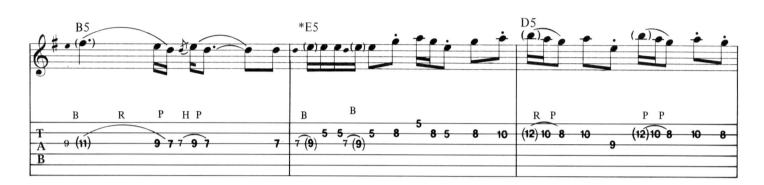

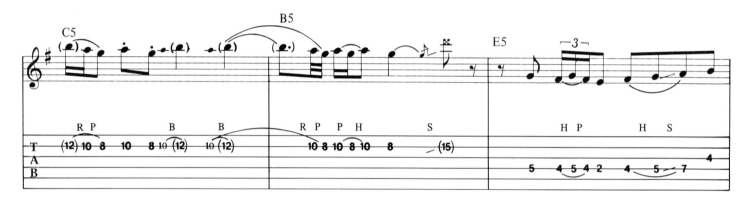

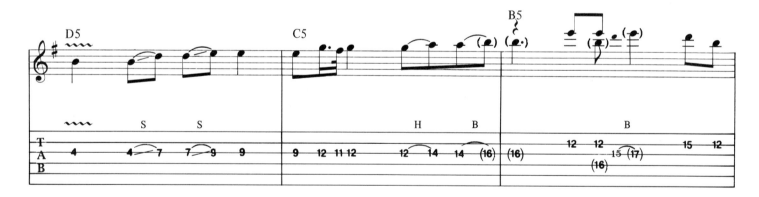

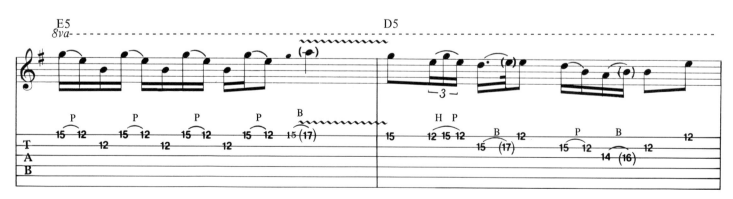

* Left channel overdub not notated.

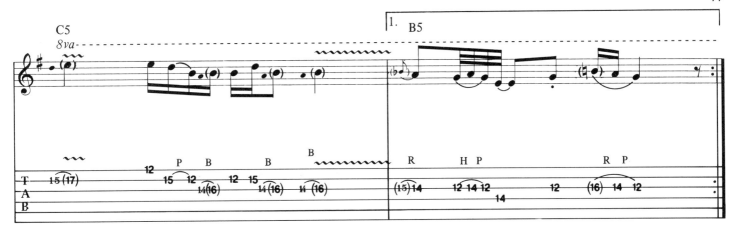

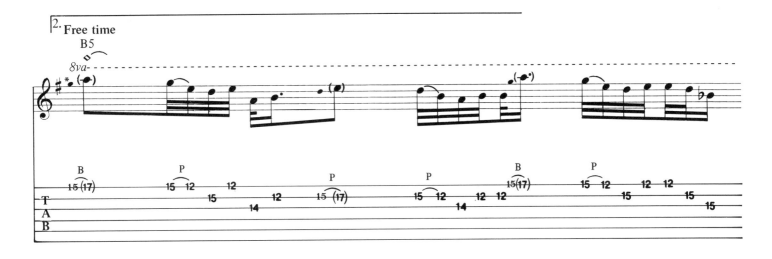

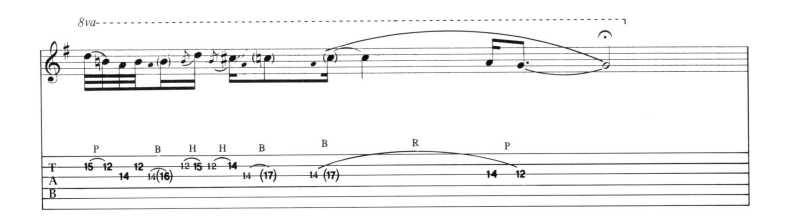

* Right channel overdub not notated

NEON KNIGHTS

Words by Ronnie James Dio/Music by Ronnie James Dio, Terence Butler, Anthony Iommi, and William Ward

Fast Rock beat

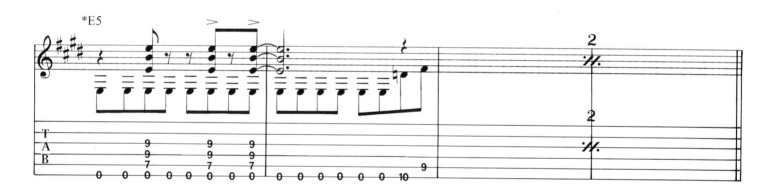

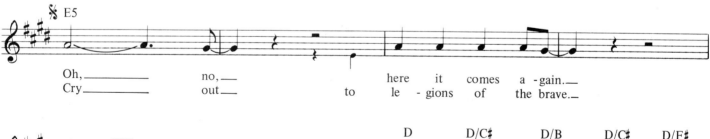

Oh, _____ no, _____ here it comes a-gain. _____

Cry _____ out _____ to le - gions of the brave. _____

Can't re - mem - ber when ___ we came so close to love be -

Time a - gain ___ to save ___ us from the close jack - als of the

fore.

street.

Hold on. _____

Ride out, _____ pro -

*E5=E (omit 3rd)

80

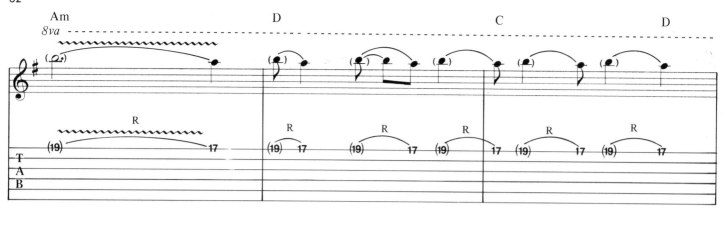

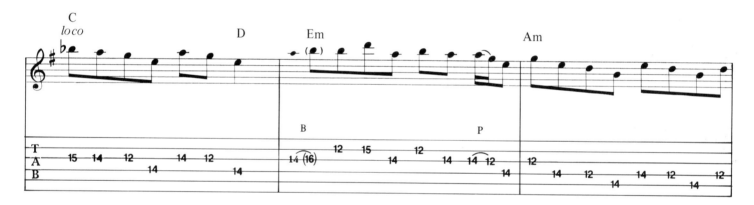

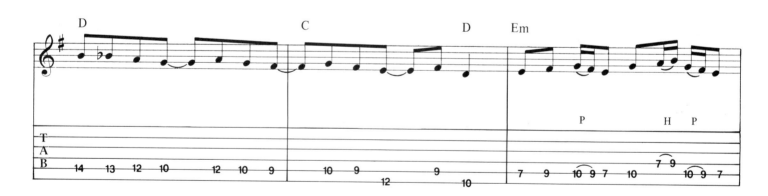

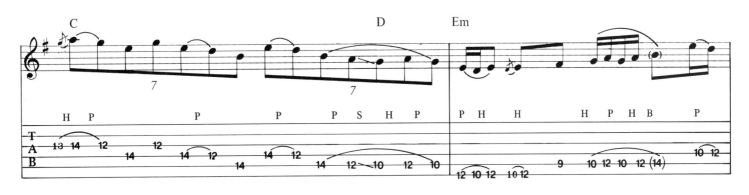

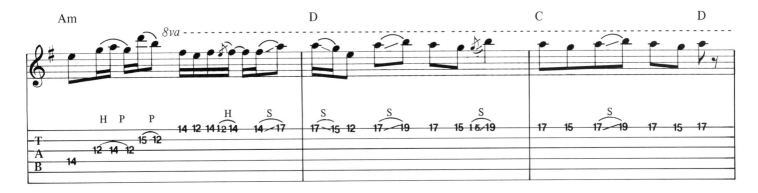

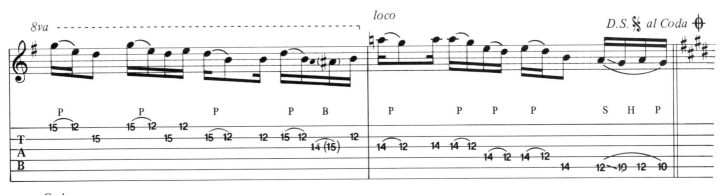

Ne - on knights,— ne - on knights,— ne - on knights.—

Repeat and fade (lead Guitar ad lib)

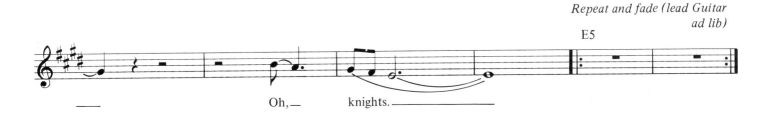

Oh,— knights.———

Never Say Die

Words and Music by Anthony Frank Iommi, Terence Butler, John Osbourne, and William Ward

*F5 = F (omit 3rd)

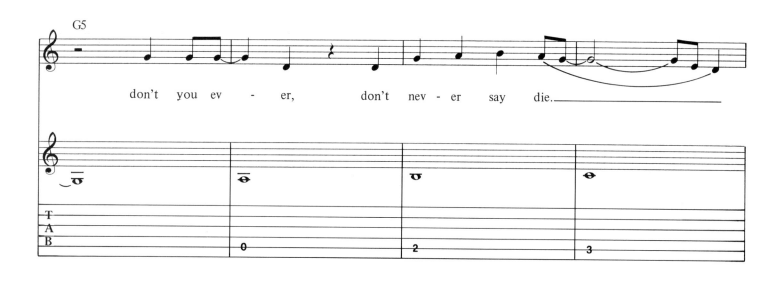

don't you ev - er, don't nev - er say die._____

Nev - er, nev - er, nev - er say die_____ a - gain._

Some -

Don't you ev - er say die. Don't

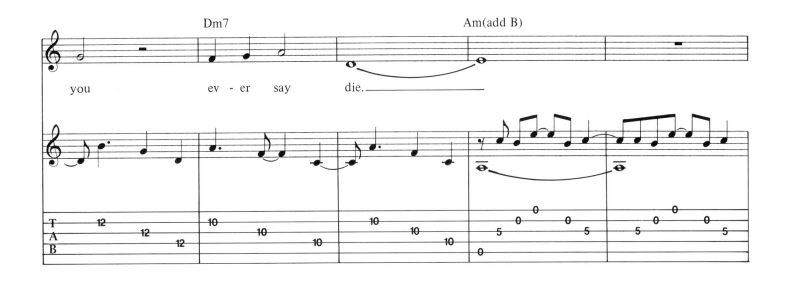

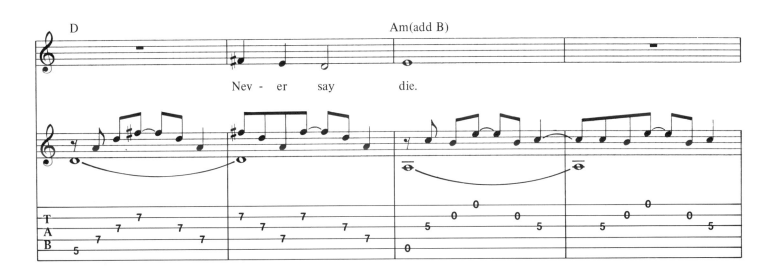

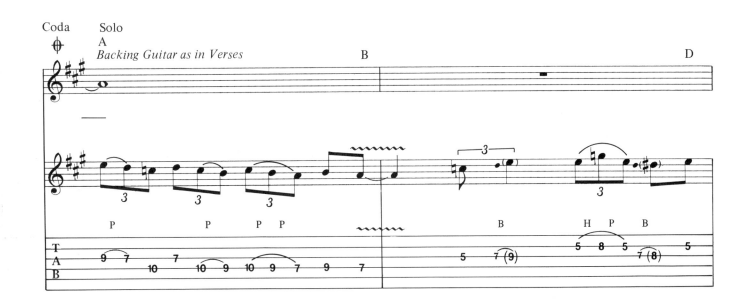

Nev- er say   die.

PARANOID

Words and Music by Anthony Iommi, John Osbourne, William Ward, and Terence Butler

* E5 = E (omit 3rd)

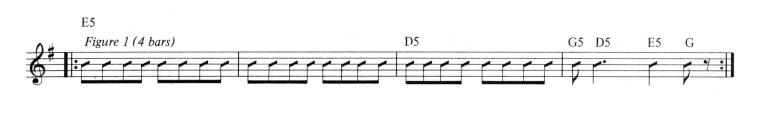

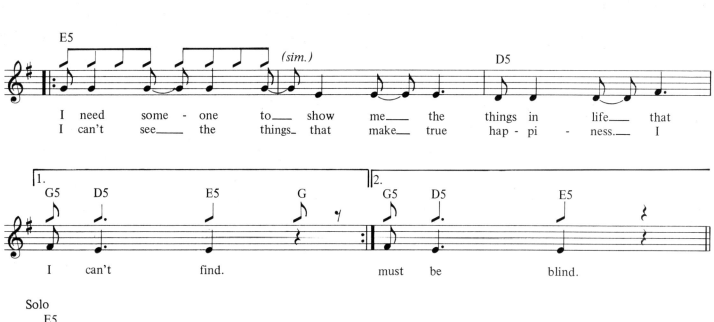

I need some - one to___ show me___ the things in life___ that
I can't see___ the things_ that make___ true hap - pi - ness.___ I

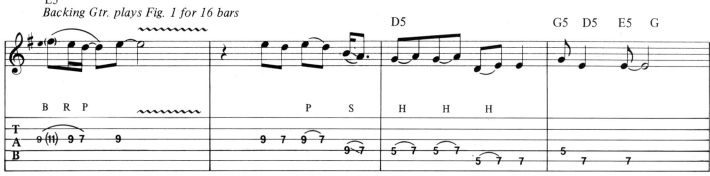

I can't find.   must be   blind.

Solo

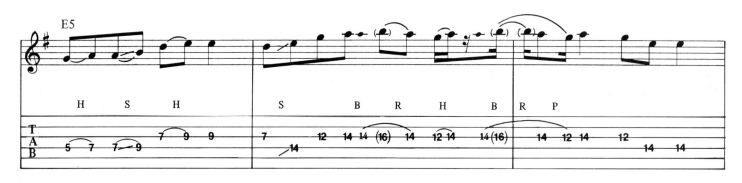

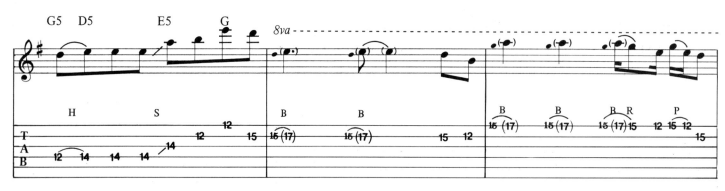

PLANET CARAVAN

Words and Music by Frank Iommi, John Osbourne, William Ward, and Terence Butler

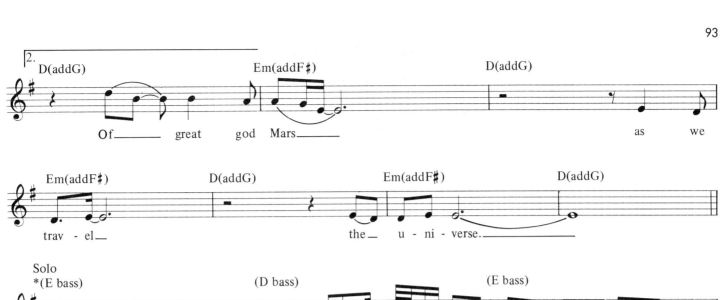

Of____ great god Mars____

trav - el____ the__ u - ni - verse.____

Solo

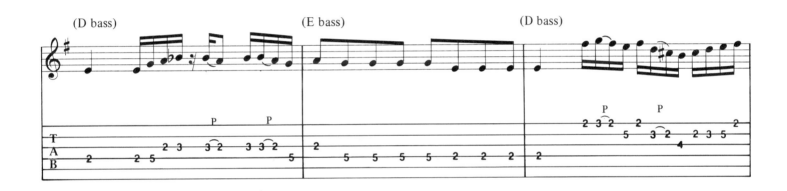

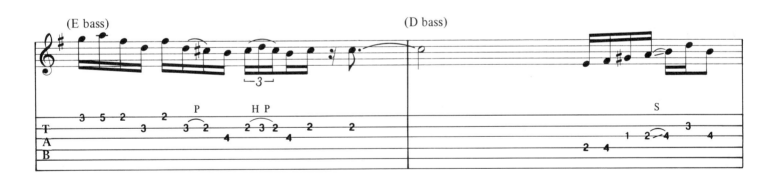

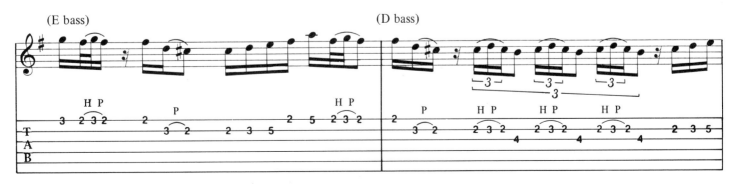

*Indicates note played by Bass Guitar only.

Fade out

SABBATH, BLOODY SABBATH

Words and Music by Frank Iommi, William Ward, Terence Butler, and John Osbourne

*To play along with recording, tune all strings down one whole step.
**D5 = D(omit 3rd)

Where can you run_____ to?
Ev - 'ry - thing a - round___ you,

Medley:
SLEEPING VILLAGE/A BIT OF FINGER
Words and Music by Frank Iommi, Terence Butler, William Ward, and John Osbourne

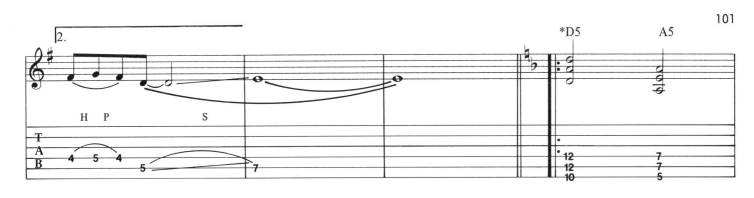

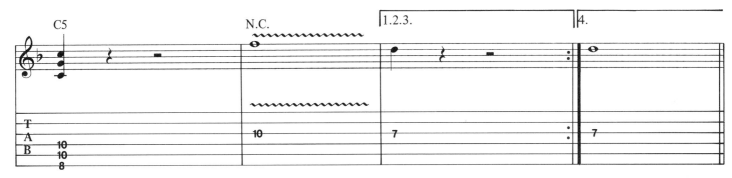

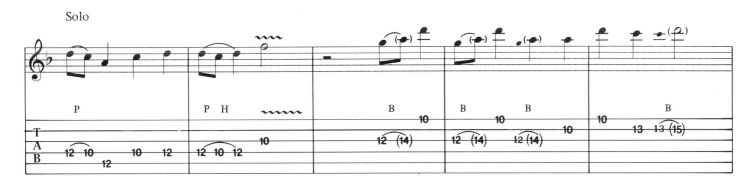

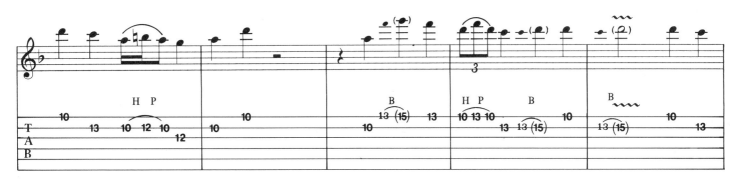

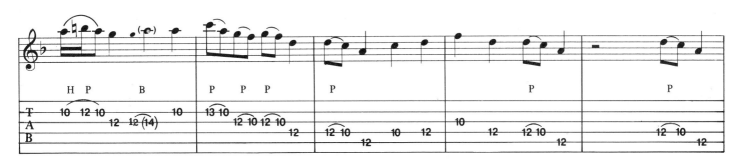

*D5 = D(omit 3rd)

** Indicates note played by Bass Guitar only

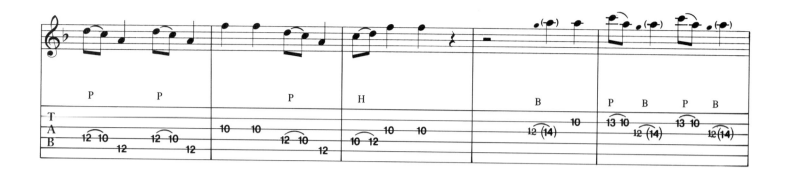

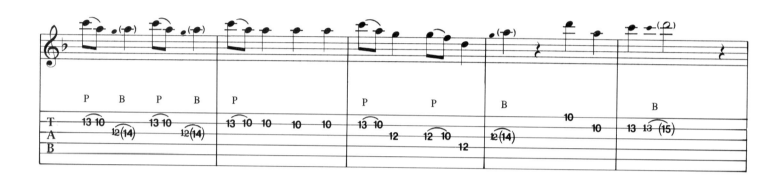

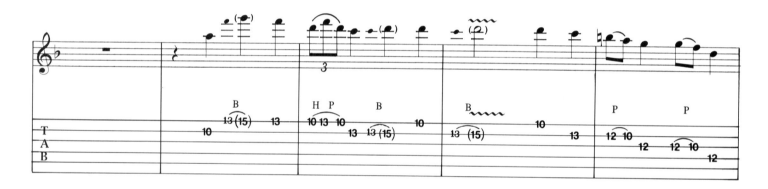

Snowblind

Words and Music by Frank Iommi, Terence Butler, William Ward, and John Osbourne

What you get and what you see,___ things that don't come eas-i-ly.___
Feel-ing hap-py in my vein,___ i-ci-cles are in my brain.___

Some-thing blow-ing in my hair;___
Death would freeze my ver-y soul;___

win-ter's ice, it soon was dead.___
makes me hap-py, makes me cold.___

*To play along with recording, tune all strings down one whole step.
**E5 = E (omit 3rd)

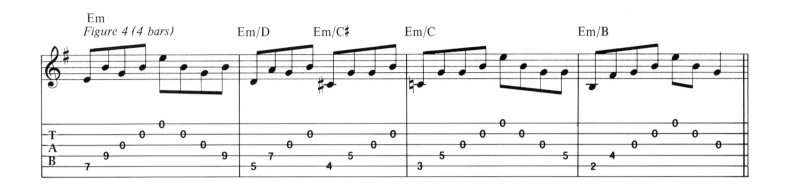

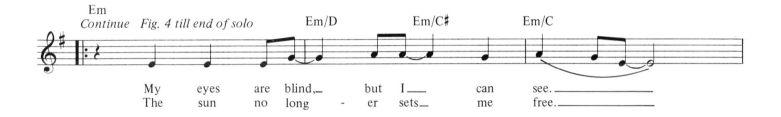

My eyes are blind,— but I___ can see.___
The sun no long - er sets__ me free.___

The snow - flakes glis - ten on__ the
I feel__ there's no place freez - ing

tree._____   me._____

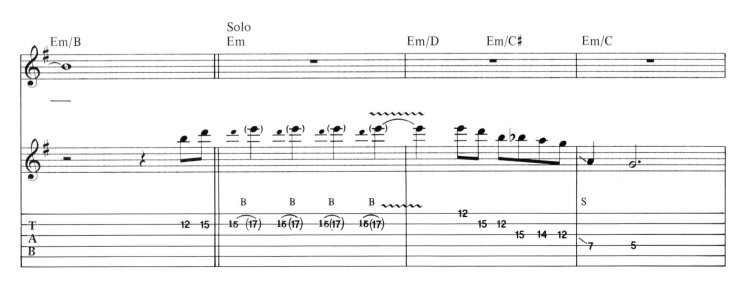

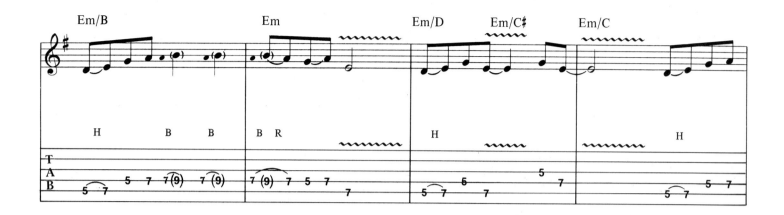

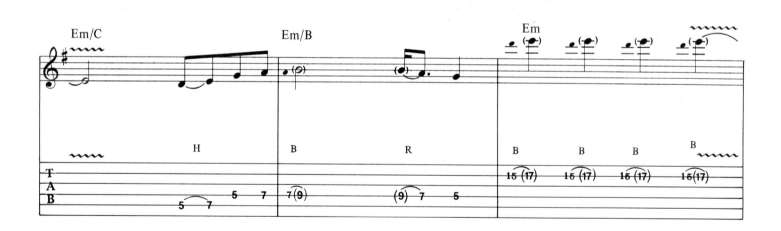

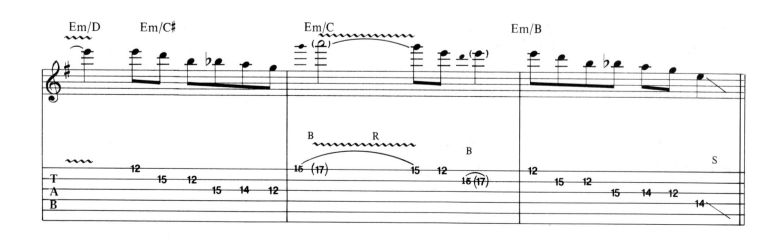

Let the win-ter sun shine on.__
Fill my dreams with flakes of snow.__

Let me feel the frost of dawn.__
Soon I'll feel the chill-ing go.__

Don't you think I know what I'm do - ing.
You're the one that's real - ly the los - er.

Don't tell me that it's do - ing me wrong.__
This is where I feel I be - long. __

Crys - tal world with win - ter flow - ers,
Ly - ing snow - blind in the sun, __

turn my days to fro - zen hours.__
will my ice age ev - er come?__

Repeat and fade
(lead Gtr. ad lib)

Supernaut

Words and Music by Frank Iommi, Terence Butler, William Ward, and John Osbourne

*C5=C (omit 3rd)

I've crossed the o-cean, turned ev-'ry bend.___ I found the cross-ing near a

gold-en rain-bow's end.___ I've been through mag-ic and through life's re-al-i-ty.___

I've lived a thou-sand years and it nev-er both-ered me.___

N.C.
Play Fig. 1 till end of Solo

Solo
N.C.

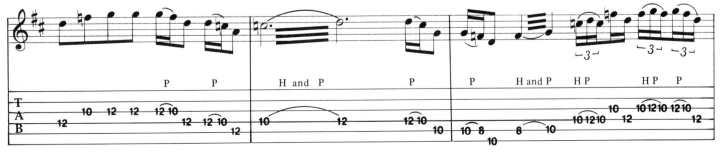

110

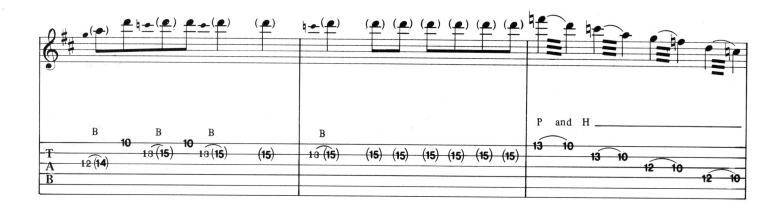
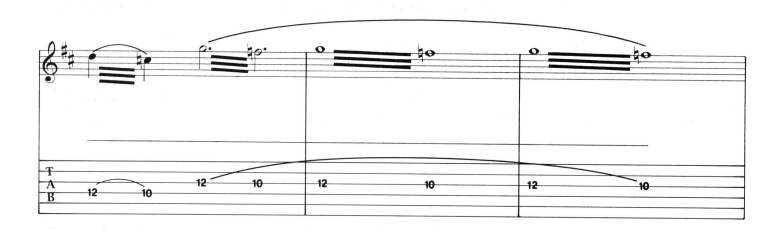
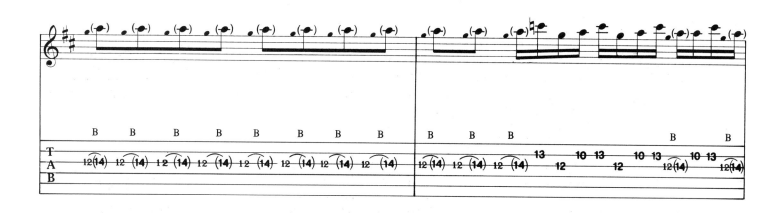
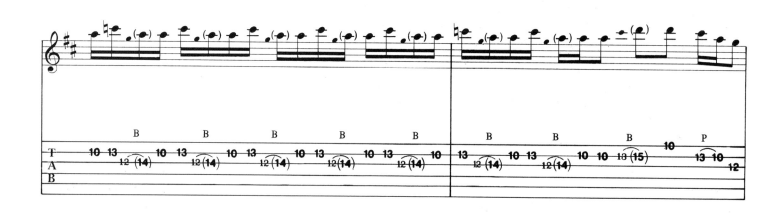

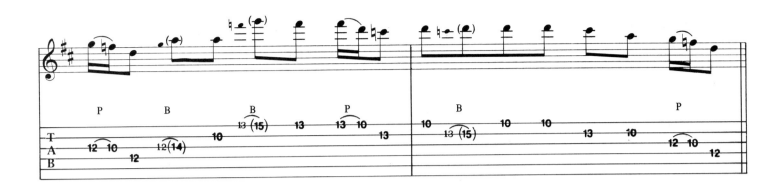

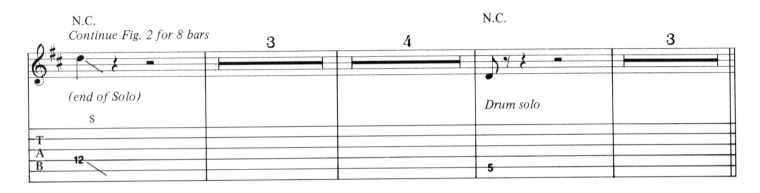

Got no re-li-gion; don't need no friends.__ Got all I want and I don't

need to pre-tend.__ Don't try to reach me 'cause I'd tear up your mind.__

I've seen the fu-ture and I've left it be-hind.____

Repeat and fade

Medley:

UNDER THE SUN/EVERY DAY COMES AND GOES

Words and Music by Frank Iommi, Terence Butler, William Ward, and John Osbourne

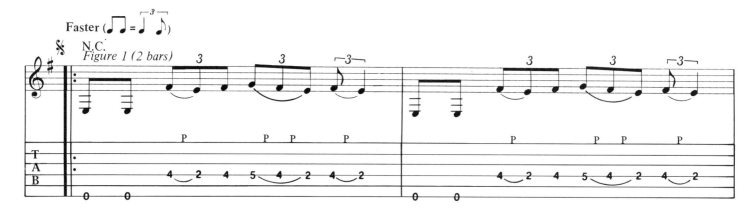

Play 3 times

Well, I don't want no Je - sus freak to
Well, I don't want no preach - er tell - ing
So be - lieve what I tell you; it's the

tell me what it's all — a - bout,—
me a - bout the God in the sky.—
on - ly way you'll find in the end.—

No
No, I don't
Just be -

black ma - gi - cian tell - ing me to cut — my soul out.—
want no one— to tell me where I'm gon - na go when I die.—
lieve in your - self.— You know you real - ly should-n't have to pre - tend.—

*To play along with recording, tune all strings down one whole step.

Don't be - lieve in vi - o - lence; I don't e - ven be - lieve _ in
I want to live my life. _ I don't want peo - ple tell - ing me what to
So let those emp - ty peo - ple try and in - ter - fere with your

peace. _ I've o - pened the door _ now, My _
do. _ I just be - lieve in my self, _ 'cause no _
mind. _ Just live your _ life _ and leave _

_ mind's been _ re - leased. _
_ one else _ is true. _
_ them all _ be - hind. _

1.   2.   *Fine*

Very fast

Ev - 'ry day _ just comes and goes. _ Life is one long o - ver - dose. _

rhythmic fig. similar

Peo - ple drive to ru - in - a - tion. I _ can see from their _ frus - tra - tion. _

(Drum fill)

*A5 = A (omit 3rd)

114

People hid - ing their real fac - es, each__ one run-ning their__ rat rac - es. Be-

hind each flow'r there grows a weed____ in their world of make be - lieve.____

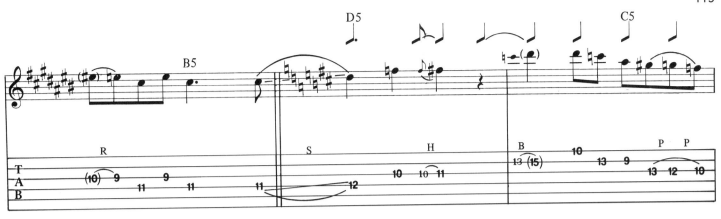

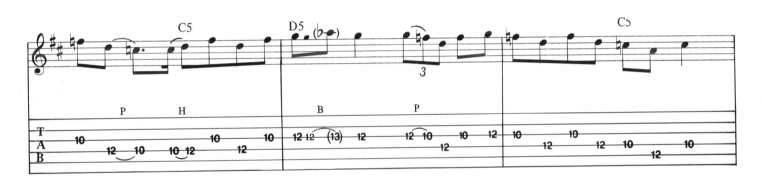

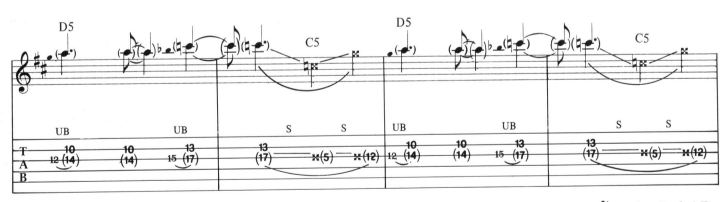

D.S. %‌ (2nd ending) al Fine

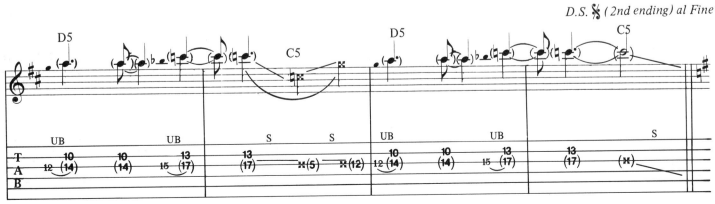

WAR PIGS

Words and Music by Frank Iommi, John Osbourne, William Ward, and Terence Butler

As the war machine keeps turn - ing.
On their knees the war pigs crawl - ing,

Death and ha - tred to man - kind,
Beg - ging mer - cies for their sins.

Poi - son - ing their brain - washed minds. Oh, Lord, yeah.
Sa - tan, laugh - ing, spreads his wings. Oh, Lord, yeah.

Figure 2 (16 bars: 4+4+4+4)

*G5

1.3.

N.C.

2.

4.

To Coda II

N.C.

*G5 = G (omit 3rd)

Play 4 times

Solo I
*(E bass)

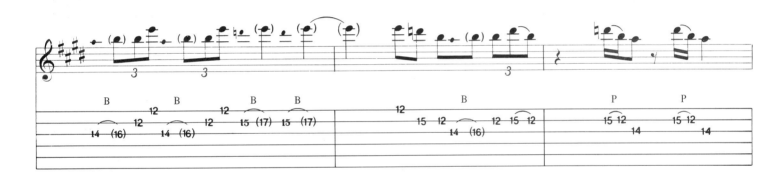

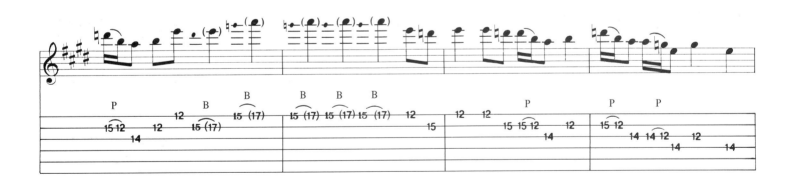

*Indicates note played by Bass Guitar only.

120

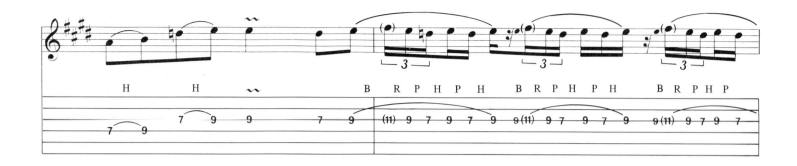

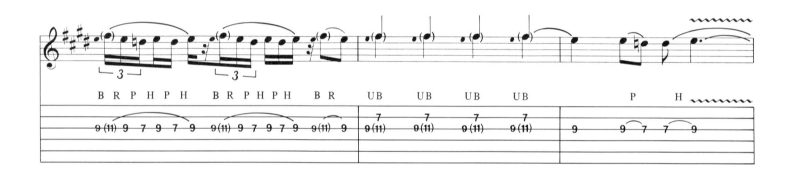

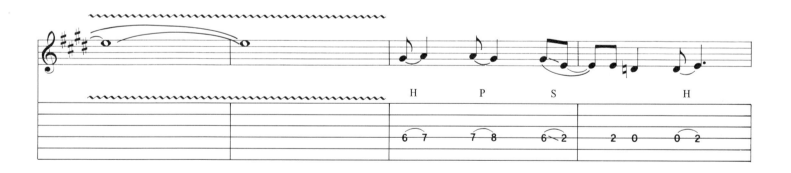

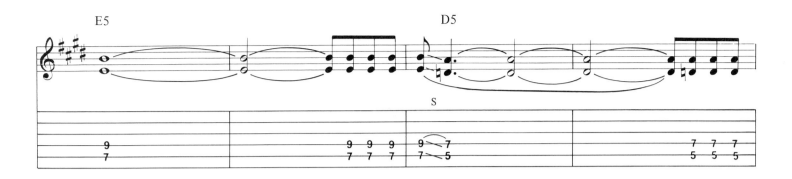

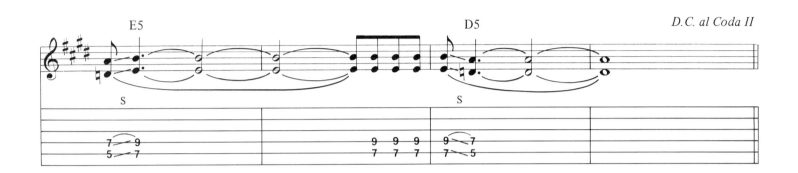

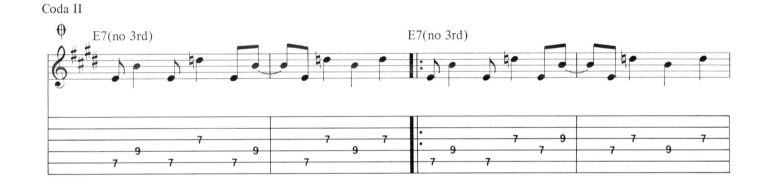

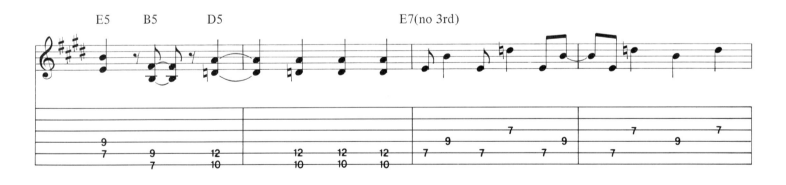

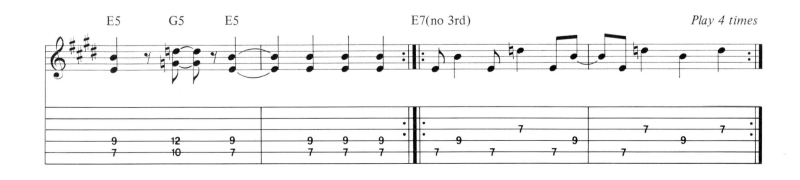

122

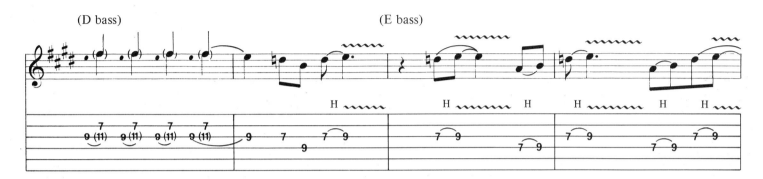

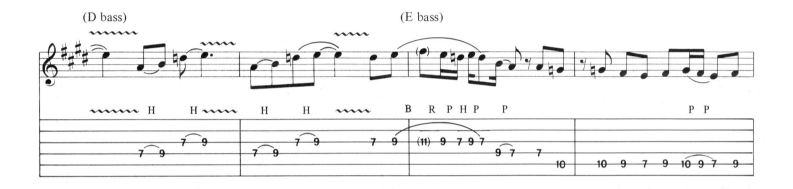

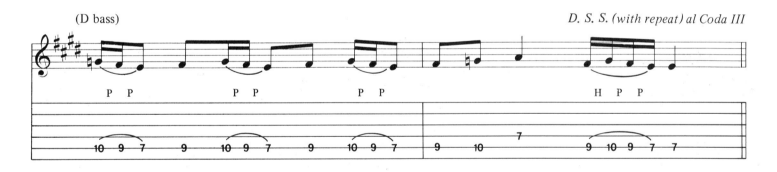

Coda III

Play 5 times (on 4th time, accel. till end)

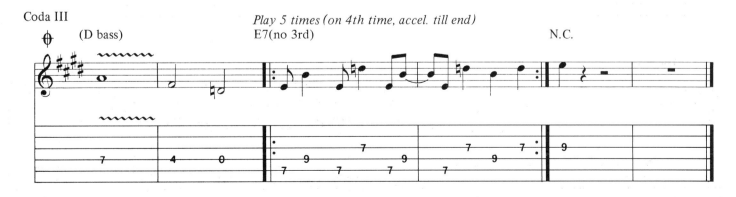

THE WIZARD

Words and Music by Frank Iommi, Terence Butler, William Ward, and John Osbourne

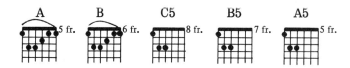

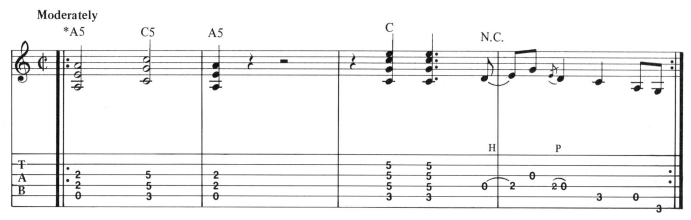

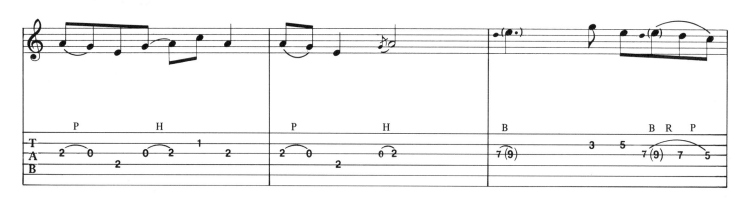

*A5 = A(omit 3rd)

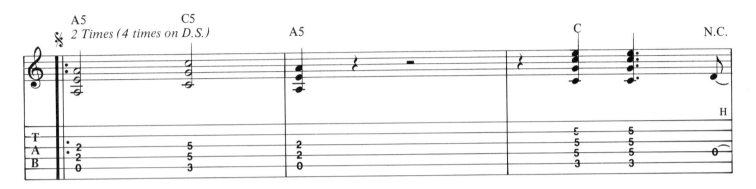

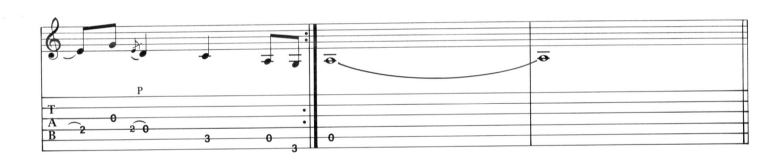

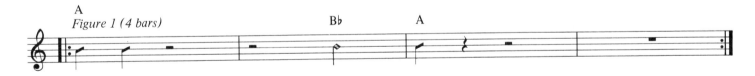

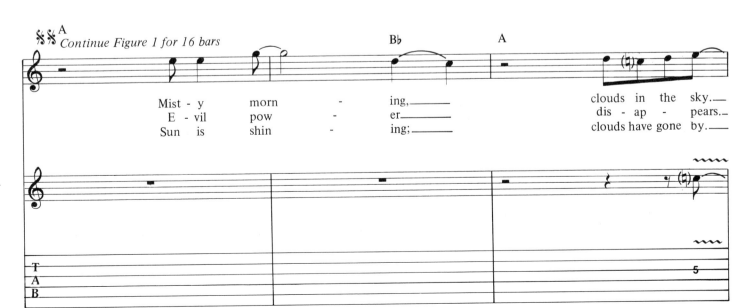

Mist - y morn - ing,_____ clouds in the sky.
E - vil pow - er_____ dis - ap - pears.
Sun is shin - ing;_____ clouds have gone by._____

Nev - er   talk - ing,—

just keeps   walk - ing,—   spread - ing his mag - ic.—

Coda I

Solo

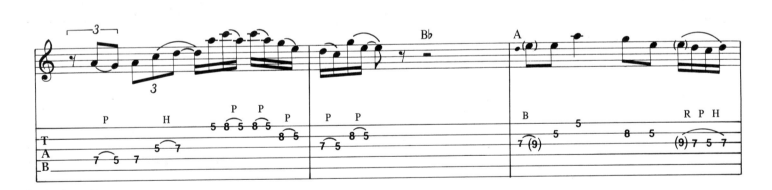

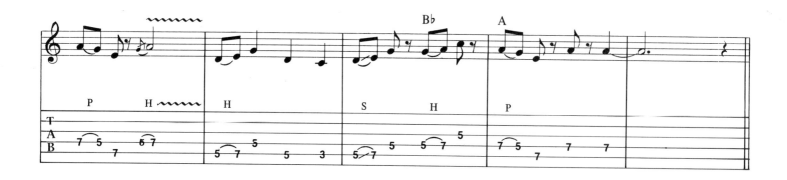

Harmonica Solo

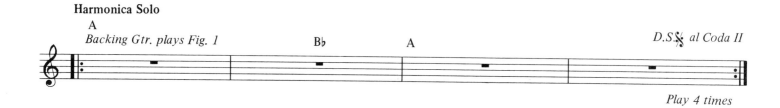

Coda II

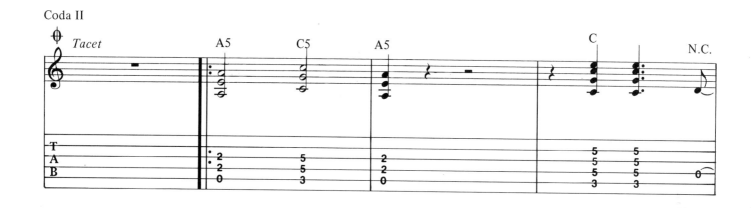

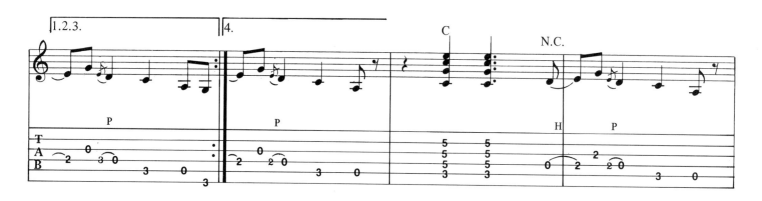